A Little Book of
EXCUSES

D0494052

A Little Book of

EXCUSES

JASMINE BIRTLES

BOXTREE

First published 2001 by Boxtree
an imprint of Pan Macmillan Ltd
Pan Macmillan, 20 New Wharf Road, London N1 9RR
Basingstoke and Oxford
Associated companies throughout the world
www.panmacmillan.com

ISBN 0 7522 6154 1

1 3 5 7 9 8 6 4 2

A CIP catalogue record for this book is available from
the British Library.

Typeset by Dan Newman/Perfect Bound Ltd
Printed by The Bath Press, Bath

Contents

I'm sorry I'm late but . . .

Late again? And the boss says that if you do it once more you'll be demoted to personnel? Try one of these. they're bound to be impressed by your creativity, if not your actual honesty.

My grandmother made a
last-minute recovery ...
and I had to hit her with a spade.

I'm very rich and my house crosses
an international dateline.

I'm sorry I'm late but...

I was waiting for the Viagra
to wear off.

I was waiting for the Prozac
to wear off.

> **I'm sorry I'm late but...**

Is that the time? Heavens, doesn't time fly when you're helping homeless, orphaned, child amputees!

9

I'm sorry I'm late but...

I was attacked twenty-five times
by a mugger with short-term
amnesia.

No, I really was caught in a bank
robbery this time. You pay me so
little I had to rob a bank.

10

I'm sorry I'm late but...

I've just come out of a breakfast
meeting with your boss.
But don't worry, I stuck up for you
the whole time.

I'm sorry I'm late but...

My teeth brace set off the alarm at
Selfridges and I was forced to
wander round the lingerie section
for hours before they let me out.

I'm still three hours earlier than yesterday – I'd call that progress, wouldn't you?

Sorry I'm late. I was ready but my inner child refused to get dressed.

I was attacked by a flock of birds who mistook dandruff for breadcrumbs.

Sorry I'm late, but I've been searching for the hero inside myself.

Sorry I'm late for the meeting but I got stuck in a porn site on the Internet and had to spend five hours going through every page before I managed to get out.

I'm sorry I'm late but...

I installed a new waterbed yesterday and when I woke up this morning I was seasick.

I passed out in the lift after being overpowered by my new perfume.

My wife was getting pregnant and I wanted to be there.

Airport security frisked me
and I enjoyed it so much I went
round again – via Rome.

I was abducted by a religious cult
who taught me punctuality
was a mortal sin.

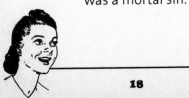

Look at it cosmically. If you see the history of the world as a day, civilization has only happened in the last few minutes. So really I'm barely a nanosecond late.

I was at the constipation awards ceremony. Do you want to see my trophy?

My dentist was kidnapped by the tooth fairy.

I have a back problem.
I can't get it off the bed.

My cat is suffering from
depression, so I've been telling
it jokes all morning.

Sorry I can't work, but . . .

Just can't be arsed to turn up today, or yesterday, or ever? Who can blame you? Well, your boss, that's who, so get the first word in.

I have a rare case of forty-eight-hour projectile leprosy.

The dog ate my car keys. We're going to hitchhike to the vet.

I suffer from SAD but I have a rare case in which I get it all year round.

I didn't take the day off, I was having an eight-hour cigarette break.

I'm still converting my calendar
from Julian to Gregorian.

Sorry I can't work, but . . .

I didn't just 'not turn up', I was assiduously following my new commitment to negative reliability.

I just found out that I was
switched at birth so I am on a
quest to find my real parents.

I thought I'd stay at home today so
that you would miss me and
discover just how valuable I am to
the firm.

I was watching breakfast television
and mysteriously lost the will
to live.

I'm finding that the job is
interfering with my drinking.

The psychiatrist thinks I'm not quite ready to face work. On the plus side, he gave me a jaw restraint so I won't bite things when I am startled.

I can't come in to work today because I'll be stalking my previous boss, who fired me for not showing up for work. OK?

My voices told me I shouldn't
turn up today.

I realize reliability is important,
but so is my need to remain
an enigma.

Sorry I can't work, but . . .

I had this great idea for resolving
the crisis in Northern Ireland
and wanted to bounce it off
Nelson Mandela.

I work on the system that every month has the same number of days and firmly believe that everyone else will eventually come round.

I've used up all my sick days . . .
so I'm calling in dead.

I thought I wanted a job but it
turns out I just want the money.

Sorry I can't work, but . . .

My cover in the witness-protection
programme has been exposed.
If I were you, I'd call the
anti-terrorist squad.

Sorry about my work . . .

Some people are so ungrateful. As if you weren't already making the supreme sacrifice by actually turning up for work, they start criticizing your behaviour once you're there. Make sure you show them who has an answer for everything.

That's never me – you couldn't fit
half my arse on an A4 photocopier.

Sorry about my work . . .

I've always had a problem
recognizing authority. For the first
six months I thought I reported to
the sandwich lady.

> **Sorry about my work . . .**

I seem to have contracted some
attention-deficit disorder, so –
why are you calling?

I'm not planning to join a
competitor, I always download
everything onto floppies and take
them home at night.

Yes, Hitler got the trains to run on time, but that's because they were going to the death camps. Rather like this office.

Sorry about my work . . .

I know the figures are bad this month, but if you gave me a rise I could afford a much better suit. Come on, it's a start, isn't it?

Let's face it, if you had provided
a designated smoking area
the office wouldn't have burned
down after I had that fag in the
ventilation shaft.

Well, yes . . . I suppose leaving
my business card in phone-boxes
could be construed as prostitution.
But look how many new clients
we got!

It's true we lost a few key accounts this year, but given how little work I did, I think the figures are highly encouraging.

No, you see my RSI affects my
computer hand, not my beer arm.

Sorry about the CV . . .

Some people are so petty. Prospective employers seem to want things like facts in your CV and some sort of relevant experience. Let them know what kind of force they're really dealing with in the interview room.

No, I haven't provided any references because my previous employers are still in the witness-protection programme.

Well, I didn't exactly graduate from Oxford, but I did pass out there a few times.

Strictly speaking those aren't my qualifications, no, but passing exams is 80% confidence anyway and I'm 90% confident I would have passed if I'd taken them.

I wouldn't say I was bad at man-management, but castration really is too good for the bastards, don't you think?

I've never been that good with figures, but hey – how hard can accountancy be?

Sorry about writing my CV on toilet paper – interviews make me *really* nervous.

Well, I don't have much commercial experience but in a previous life I used to run Microsoft.

No, strictly speaking I'm not qualified for the job, but in my favour I do get drunk easily and clothes just fall off these shoulders.

I don't see why they had to stop the job interview. I only asked if they ever pressed charges.

> # Sorry about the sex . . .

Hmm. I think we all know what we're talking about here.

Sorry, I'm not used to being with a woman I don't have to inflate.

Hold on – are you recording this?
No? Well, I am.

> **Sorry about the sex . . .**

The thing is, I feel intimidated
because you're good enough to do
this for a living.

I only slept with her because she
reminded me of you. How was I to
know she was your sister?

Sorry about the sex . . .

Yes, we did sleep together but I
swear I never stopped looking at
my watch. Compared to you it
seemed to go on for hours.

Ooh, touchy! I only asked if you
wanted to make £50
lying on your back.

I don't deserve you, so I thought
I'd try someone else.

Sorry about the sex . . .

I'm smiling because I never used to win anything when I was a kid, but now I come first every time!

Yes, sometimes my mother *does* write little notes saying 'Can't wait to do it again, you hot lover'. What of it?

> **Sorry about the sex . . .**

It's not a love-bite, it's a rare form
of joined-up measles.

I plead insanity. I'd have to be mad
to do it with her.

Of course my one-night stand isn't hiding in the cupboard! Since when can you get the All Blacks in a cupboard?

Oh, how rude of me. This is my boyfriend, and this . . . is a homeless person to whom I offered a bed for the night.

> **Sorry about the sex . . .**

We weren't making love, we were
horizontally networking.
Don't you know *anything*
about e-commerce?

It's not lipstick on my collar, there was a teenager next to me on the train, and his spot exploded.

A love letter? No, this is someone's idea of a cruel joke – and to hide it in the bottom of my pants drawer?!

It's not a girl's phone number.
It's her VAT number.

Sorry, I'm just not used to doing
this with someone else.

She meant nothing to me . . . other
than a night of wild passion that I
will remember to the end of my
days and against which I will
measure all other women.

Sorry I'm such a crap lover . . .

Some people are so demanding. They want things like love, affection and even your physical presence sometimes. Keep them in their place before they demand even more – like knowing your name or something.

I'm a busy executive. I can't be
expected to remember everything.
What did you say our child's
name was?

I don't flirt with everyone – mind
you, I haven't met everyone yet.

It only *looks* cheap. Actually it's a very expensive ring and was designed by one of those modern *ironic* jewellers.

I can't meet you because ugly people make me physically sick and I don't want to mess up your clothes.

If you think I've come in smelling of another woman then your nostrils must have given out.

Daniella!

Sorry I'm such a crap lover . . .

That was no romantic clinch.
Don't you anything about the
Heimlich manoeuvre?

All right, I am dumping you, but look at it this way, a couple of years ago I wouldn't even have given someone like you a second look, let alone gone out with you.

I did send you flowers direct from Amsterdam, but they must have got caught in customs.

Sorry I'm such a crap lover . . .

It was my camera and I just
thought photos like that ought to
be enjoyed by thousands of lonely
men who can reach the top shelf.

How was I to know *Kiss my Whip*
wasn't a film about cookery?

I know I said I'd stay with you.
I just didn't say for how long.

I would have taken you to the party but I knew it would be full of the beautiful people and I didn't want you to feel left out.

Didn't I tell you at the ceremony
I wanted an open marriage?

I just didn't hate myself enough
to go out with you.

Sorry I'm such a crap lover . . .

I was going to write but they won't let us have anything sharp in here.

I can't go back to your place. Two people won't fit under a rock.

I'm sorry I pulled your nose. I
thought you were wearing a
Hallowe'en mask.

Sorry about the housework . . .

Charity begins at home so do your bit – patronize everyone and then feel good about yourself by slipping them a fiver once a year.

I couldn't wash up because I'm allergic to cleaning products. And cutlery. Oh, and the doctor said I should avoid plates, too.

I'm not lazy, my chiropractor says I have to work lying down.

I can't tidy my bedroom. I'm entering it for the Turner prize.

Well, it's called a dryer and it doesn't say 'not for puppies' so how was I to know?

I'm donating my brain to science
and I don't want it to be too worn
by the time they get it.

I did mean to put the shelves up but I was watching *Changing Rooms* and life just lost all meaning.

It's not *my* fault. You should have looked in the oven before you turned it on.

How was I to know it was alive? It didn't struggle when I flushed it.

Sorry I'm a criminal . . .

So you've done a bit of arson and aggravated assault. So? Who hasn't? Don't let a little blue light put you off your stride.

Honestly, I'm not under the affluence of incohol, ossifer.

I wasn't speeding; I was trying to disprove the laws of momentum.

What do you mean, officer, 'Have you been drinking?' You're the trained observer.

I was trying to keep up with the other traffic. Yes, I know there is no other car around, that's how far ahead of me they are.

Sorry, officer, I didn't realize my radar detector wasn't plugged in.

You can write as many tickets as you like. I stole the car anyway.

You may call it speeding but I think you'll find that 80 m.p.h. is hardly Mach one.... Yes, I am known as a pedant.

It's an inishish ceremony . . . it's an initiashash ceremony . . . OK, I'm pissed.

Sorry, mate . . .

Friends, family and other reptiles.
They're all after your blood. Still,
you have to throw a sop to them
sometimes.

> **Sorry, mate . . .**

I was going to write earlier
but I've been snowed under.
PS: Sorry to hear about your death.

Well, I would have been there but something came up at the last minute. Ditto the wedding, reception and honeymoon. Divorce.

> **Sorry, mate . . .**

So Happy Christmas!
Sorry I wasn't there but I got the
dates mixed up – December 25th,
you say?

I wasn't spreading gossip, but I
know someone who is . . .

I didn't forget our anniversary,
I just figured why go out for a meal
with the guy when you're about to
dump him and tell all his friends?

I swear I was on my way to the hospital, and then I thought, 'Heart bypass . . . better wear black, eh? Just in case.'

Look, you were always complaining
that he was a useless husband.
I've just taken him off your hands.
After all, what are best friends for?

I didn't forget your birthday,
I just didn't want to remind you
of your wasted life.

It was his last wish that I attend
the funeral as Ronald McDonald.

> # Whenever, whatever . . .

Sometimes the deeper the mess, the easier the excuse. No one will forgive you anyway, so why bother being creative?

I didn't take your money. It was just resting in my account.

Am I drunk?
The problem is you're not.

Is it really my round?
Oh, I've just put all my spare cash
in the charity jar.

I'd like to help and I would too if it
weren't for this damned coma.

Don't worry, I forgot
your name too.

I'm sorry, I can't hear you.
I'm deaf and dumb.

I'm not gossiping –
it's called 'knowledge sharing'.

I'd stay and talk but there are so
many more interesting people in
the world.

Look, when you vacuum in the nude it's easy to slip, and yes, the nozzle was pointing upwards.

I need ten hours' sleep a day.
Eight at night.

The cheque's in the post.
No, really, I stuck it in a crack
in a gatepost.

Well, it says 'all you can eat'.
It doesn't say the kitchen's out
of bounds.

You want money!
But I thought teenagers *liked*
to be paid in cocaine.

But you said you liked to get
stoned at the weekend. How was
I to know you meant drugs?

I *was* revising. Westlife's lyrics have a direct bearing on the issues surrounding the Reform Act of 1832.

I wasn't lying. I was being
economical with the truth.

If I told you I'd have to kill you.

I'm not really a priest,
I just love hearing gossip
through a wire mesh.

The dog ate my homework.
So I ate the dog.

We weren't rubbish. The Accrington Stanley under 13s Second Eleven are a hard nut to crack.

I'm afraid we had to put Mr Frisky down. He didn't suffer . . . in fact, if you rush to the window he's probably still falling . . .

Sorry about the politics . . .

Friends, Romans, countrymen,

lend me your excuses.

I'm sorry you haven't had a reply to your complaint but here at the council we find it's far more efficient to recycle letters through the wastebins before they're even opened.

I used to be a policeman, so when they passed me the baton I naturally started beating the other athletes with it.

Look, Tony, if I'd known she was the
Queen Mother, do you honestly
think I'd have chinned her?

Well Mr President, I thought
we've taken the space shuttle into
orbit so many times – hell, let's fly
over Vegas!

So, Mr Mandela – sorry about that
lost paperwork that kept you in
prison for thirty-five years . . .

As President, I realize I should have set a better example, and I apologize. But while I'm here, if there's anyone who fancies doing it on Air Force One, I'm your man!

Ooh, Matron.

Really, Doctor, you said
prick his boils?

Look, it's called a heart–lung bypass – so swapping them around is bound to work.

Well, you know, there's big money in kidneys and I figured you had two of them, so as you were under the knife anyway . . .

Yes, the item found its way inside
you during the op but think of it
this way: at least the alarm only
goes off once a day.

Well no, strictly speaking I haven't
actually done heart surgery before
but I am a big fan of *ER*.

Jasmine Birtles was voted 'Woman of the Year' by the reader of the *Embalmer's Gazette* in 1983. She is known as a tough woman who's not afraid to fire people, even if they don't work for her. Once voted 'Girl most likely to chin herself' by the 1922 Committee, she set up a mobile hairdressing salon in the House of Lords and was eventually honoured for services to leg-waxing. She then worked for the Body Shop and was responsible for introducing Avocado and House Marten Foot Balm and Guava and Cheeseburger Hair Conditioner. She has webbed feet and is a founder member of the Synchronized Proctocolgy Study Circle.